With unwavering devotion

To Adaiah and Josh on their wedding day with love...

From Kent and Linda

simple truths for

FRIENDS

new seasons™
a division of Publications International, Ltd.

Original inspirations by:
Georgann Freeman, Margaret Anne Huffman, Marie Jones.

Photo credits:
Front cover: FPG International: Barbara Peacock.
FPG International: Gary Buss; Dana Edmunds; Barbara Peacock; Richard Price; G. Randall;
Ken Ross; Mark Scott; Telegraph Colour Library; Arthur Tilley; VCG; SuperStock.

Louis Weber, CEO
Publications International, Ltd.
7373 North Cicero Avenue
Lincolnwood, Illinois 60712

THE WEIGHT OF the world
on your shoulders becomes
proportionately less to
the strength of your
friendships.

simple truths: friend

simple truths: friend

ENCOURAGEMENT FROM A friend after trouble
is as welcome as sunshine after a storm.

FRIENDS HELP LIGHT our way
during dark moments.

A CANDLE MAY light
the darkness, but a friend
will light your life.

simple truths: friend

ENDURING FRIENDSHIP IS characterized
by an open heart and an open hand.

FRIENDS KNOW THAT sometimes
the best way to be there for each other
is to communicate with silence.

TEA AND FRIENDSHIPS are available
in many comforting varieties.

FRIENDSHIP, LIKE AN heirloom pewter teapot or vintage
walnut table around which good friends gather,
grows more lovely and valuable in
the hands of daily use.

FRIENDSHIP IS AS steadying as a hand
on the rudder of a boat and as reliable
as sunrise after night.

A CALL, A NOTE, or a handclasp from a friend nudges
aside worry and loneliness just as fog lifting
on mountains peels away lingering doubts
that the summit might not be there.

simple truths: friend

A TRUE FRIEND has a knack for knowing when
you need to have a good laugh and when
you need to have a good cry.

A GOOD FRIEND is like an acrobat
who bends over backward and stands on her head
to turn your frown upside down.

simple truths: friend

simple truths: friend

FRIENDS DON'T LET friends give up.
They cheer you on even when you're failing.
They sing your praises even if you're feeling low.
Friends don't let friends give up hope.

A TRUE FRIEND may live in another state,
or even another country, but is always
only a heartbeat away.

NO AMOUNT OF time or distance can come between good friends. There is a bond that stays strong no matter the months or miles between two people who call each other "friend."

LONG-TIME FRIENDSHIP IS
the rarest of all treasures,
spilling over like foam on
the surf to flow across all
of those who are fortunate
enough to be in its path.

FRIENDSHIP DOESN'T HAVE to be fancy.
A Sunday matinee, a walk on the beach, a long talk
over a glass of homemade ice tea. It's the quality
of the time that counts.

BEST FRIENDS WALK through life together,
side by side, facing forward. Though they may each
be on a separate path, they are always traveling
in the same general direction.

simple truths: friend

FRIENDSHIP LIFTS THE heart just as sunshine
turns the flowers skyward.

NOTHING CHASES AWAY a gloomy day
like going out on the town with a bunch of good friends.
The noise, chatter, and laughter serve as the perfect medicine
to heal a lonely heart and lift a drooping spirit.

THE STRONGEST, MOST enduring friendships occur when change is welcome, growth is encouraged, and independence is supported. The bonds of friendship should never be constricting, but instead provide an ever-transforming environment of love, trust, and inspiration.

YOU DON'T PICK your friends so much as they find you.
You don't create friendship so much
as it unfolds naturally.

WE HAVE TO be so many things to so many different people in our lives, but to our friends we can be ourselves.

simple truths: friend

simple truths: friend

HAVING A FRIEND who believes in you is like
owning a second pair of wings. Their faith adds to your own,
creating a jet stream of support that carries you farther
toward the achievement of your dreams.

A FRIEND IS a keeper of secrets
and a guardian of confidences.

FRIENDSHIP IS WOVEN from vibrant
strands of loyalty, kindness, and warmth like
color-rich embroidery on a sampler.

IF NOT FOR the wealth of our friendships,
indeed we would be poor.

HAPPINESS MAY BE a warm puppy,
but joy is having a good friend to
share your life with.

simple truths: friend

SUCCESS AND GOOD
fortune mean so much
more when shared
with friends.

A FRIEND APPLAUDS your strengths,
understands your weaknesses, and appreciates
the combination that is you.

FRIENDSHIP IS ONE of the world's natural wonders. You can't force it or make it work. It has a life, and a heart, of its own.

A GOOD FRIEND is someone who knows
what's on your mind, even when
you haven't said a word.

BEST FRIENDS SHARE
clothing, food,
hopes and fears,
secrets, dreams,
worries and cares,
ideas, gossip,
advice tried and true,
laughter, tears
and recipes, too!

A DEAR FRIEND is wealth added to your
treasure chest of experiences.

A RICH PERSON has many treasures;
a wise person treasures many friendships.

FRIENDSHIP COVERS THE lives of those it touches just as a mustard seed does a Scottish hillside, laughingly paying no attention to its tiny size.

A REAL FRIEND is someone who wants to see you

succeed just as much as you do.

simple truths: friend